Alienation, Spectacle and Revolution

Alienation, Spectacle and Revolution

A critical Marxist essay

Neil Faulkner

The fast-accelerating world crisis is driving us towards barbarism and extinction. The capitalist system means ecological and social collapse. Mainstream politics, embedded in the system, has been reduced to irrelevance. Revolution has become an existential imperative. This book offers critical Marxist thinking about the nature of the crisis and what must be done to turn mass protest into the revolutionary transformation on which our survival depends.

Neil Faulkner is a writer, political theorist, revolutionary activist, and leading member of Anti*Capitalist Resistance. His books include *A Radical History of the World* (Pluto, 2018), *A People's History of the Russian Revolution* (Pluto, 2017), *Creeping Fascism: what it is and how to fight it* (Public Reading Rooms, 2017), and *System Crash: an activist guide to the coming democratic revolution* (Resistance Books, 2021).

Alienation, Spectacle, and Revolution
A critical Marxist essay

Neil Faulkner

Published 2021
Resistance Books, London
info@resistancebooks.org
www.resistancebooks.org

Cover design by Adam Di Chiara

ISBN: 978-0-902869-35-6 (print)
ISBN: 978-0-902869-34-9 (e-book)

CONTENTS

CONTENTS

Billy (Dennis Hopper): We can't even get into a second-rate hotel. I mean a second-rate motel, dig. They think we'd cut their throat. They're scared.

George (Jack Nicholson): They're not scared of you. They're scared of what you represent to them.

Billy: All we represent to them is somebody who needs a haircut.

George: Oh, no. What you represent to them is freedom. Freedom's what it's all about. Oh yeah, that's right. That's what it's all about. But talking about it and being it, that's two different things. It's real hard to be free when you are bought and sold in the marketplace. Don't tell anybody that they're not free, because they'll get busy, killing and maiming to prove to you that they are. They're going to talk to and talk to you about individual freedom. But they see a free individual, it's going to scare them. Well, it doesn't make them running scared. It makes them dangerous.

Easy Rider (1969)

Prologue: The Wall

1.

The Wall now spanned the globe. It comprised ten billion screens. Little ones, personal ones, carried in pocket or bag, to be sprung into use any spare minute, every spare minute. Big ones, able to fill a stadium with light and sound, watched by tens of thousands at a time. And all sorts of medium ones in between, laptops, X-boxes, big-screen TVs, cinema screens, and the like.

Ten billion screens. Click. Billions of images to choose from. Click. Available 24/7. Click. Whatever you want, wherever you want, whenever you want, instantly, on demand. Click.

The 7.5 billion spectators gawping at the Wall were not so much watching it as being mesmerised by it. The Wall was a tranquiliser. The spectators were already semi-comatose, otherwise they would have been doing something else, not just gawping and clicking. But once it had their attention, the Wall held them fast. It became an addiction. They couldn't drag themselves away, couldn't stop gawping and clicking. They were hooked by the eternal search for the *spectacle* – another *spectacle*, the next *spectacle*, a bigger and better *spectacle*, an as-yet-undiscovered *spectacle*.

A moment's distraction from the Wall and the gnawing FOMO began. How long before the next fix?

Always back to the Wall. Before it, an ocean of blank faces and inert bodies uploading *spectacles* into vacant brains, more and more of them, forever and ever. Until the Wall had sucked out all that remained of the life force, extinguishing mind, will, activity, freedom, reducing the spectators to husks.

2.

Marx and Engels explained how the dominant ideas in every epoch are the ideas of the ruling class, because the ruling class controls the means of production and the state, and therefore the social superstructure, and therefore the primary systems of communication, socialisation, and indoctrination – churches, schools, press, etc.

But they also argued that ideas were formed and consolidated in a more profound way. They distinguished between *appearance* and *essence* – how individuals experienced life in an everyday sense as opposed to how that experience was actually created by hidden forces. Marx's most famous example concerned labour for capital. Workers appeared to enter into a free contract with the capitalist, selling their labour-power in return for a wage that represented 'a fair day's work for a fair day's wage'. But in fact, the employment contract obscured an unequal exchange, for the worker, lacking both means of production and means of subsistence of her own, was compelled to sell her labour-power to the capitalist; and the capitalist would employ her only on condition that the value of the labour she performed both covered her wages and yielded a surplus/profit over and above that.

Nor was this, for the capitalist, a matter of

choice: he was compelled, under the whip of competition, to exploit workers in order to keep costs and prices down, to accumulate a surplus fund, to invest in more advanced techniques, to raise productivity and output; if he did not do this, he was liable to be priced out of the market by more dynamic rivals. The capitalist was, therefore, a 'personification of capital' – a living embodiment of the imperative to exploit and accumulate.

In these and other ways, social relationships between human-beings became 'thing-like'. Instead of human-beings entering freely into collective processes of creative labour, their activity was determined by forces – capital accumulation, commodity exchange, the market – outside their control. Marx used the term *reification* to describe this thing-like character of human relationships under capitalism.

The *essence* of humanity as a species is that we engage in conscious, collective, collaborative, creative labour, both in production and reproduction: we are social animals. *Reification* therefore involves an existential rupture in humanity's *species-being*. Marx used the term *alienation* to describe this rupture. Human-beings are alienated from nature, from each other, from the labour process, from the products of their labour, from their *species-being*, because of the reified character of social relations under capitalism.

The Wall is an extreme expression of *alienation*.

3.

Antonio Gramsci paid particular attention to the systems of communication, socialisation, and indoctrination by which capitalist social relations were obscured, legitimised, and sustained. He underlined the distinction between active *coercion* (by state repression) and passive *consent* (by means of socialisation, indoctrination, etc) in suppressing resistance to the system.

He saw the dominant ideas of the ruling class as a pervasive ideological *hegemony* that penetrated the whole of civil society – state, media, school, church, neighbourhood, family, etc – reaching into all the nooks and crannies of everyday life. He was struck by the way – in contrast to more ob-

viously coercive social orders like Tsarist Russia –
in which modern, developed, liberal-parliamentary
democracies acquired multi-layered ideological de-
fences against revolution from below.

This included the bureaucratised, routinised,
reformist character of most working-class organisations – trade unions and socialist parties – where
a layer of full-time functionaries operated to me-
diate between capital and labour, to contain popular revolt, to accommodate demands from below
to the imperatives of the system. They became per-
sonifications of the prevailing ideological *hegemony* inside the labour movement. They became
labour lieutenants of capital.

The Wall, the most powerful communications
system in history, is a superlative mechanism for
transmitting the hegemonic ideas of the ruling
class, sedating social discontent, suffocating dissent, achieving *consent*.

4.

The Frankfurt School was also much concerned with capitalism's mechanisms for achieving legitimation and consent, and, more broadly, for tranquilising and pacifying a potentially rebellious working class. In particular, in *One-Dimensional Man* (1964), Herbert Marcuse argued that advanced (post-war) industrialism had created an affluent consumer society in which *false needs* were created by mass media, the sales effort, popular culture, etc. Satisfaction of these needs through the consumption of commodities became a substitute for human happiness, but also a realm of unfreedom and social control which shrivelled the space for critical thought and action.

Marcuse (and others) elevated the commodity to a new theoretical level. Marx had stressed the contradictory combination of *use-value* and *exchange-value* in the capitalist commodity. On the one hand, the commodity corresponded to a real human need; on the other, it represented an objectified form of labour to be sold for profit. Marcuse, on the other hand, emphasised the rising proportion of commodities which lacked any real *use-*

value, which in fact corresponded to artificially generated *false needs*.

Capital benefitted in two senses. On the one hand, *false needs* created a growing market for consumer goods and therefore expanded capital accumulation. On the other, the satisfaction of *false needs* legitimised the system and pacified the working class; it fostered a world of atomised individual consumption, a retreat from the collective and creative into a realm of *false consciousness* and private unfulfillment and unfreedom.

False needs created a second layer of *alienation*. In Marx's conception, the worker is alienated from the *use-values* created by her labour. In Marcuse's conception, the worker is often conned into consuming commodities devoid of any real *use-value* at all.

But the Wall represents yet another layer of *alienation*.

5.

In *The Society of the Spectacle* (1967), Guy Debord argued that the world of the real – real things and real activities – had been replaced by a world of mere representations or *spectacles*. Life was no longer lived, it was merely depicted. Humans were no longer active creators of a real material world, but passive spectators of a constructed world of images.

Some of Debord's formulations were exaggerated. Human-beings are organic life-forms. They have a material existence and therefore material needs. We cannot be reduced to consumers of *spectacles*.

But, like Marcuse, Debord offered a profound insight into the deepening *alienation* characteristic of late capitalism. Where Marcuse had emphasised *false needs*, commodification, the consumer society, Debord highlighted the role of representation, images, *spectacles* in the context of growing atomisation, privatisation, and passivity.

Debord anticipated the Wall – a virtual Wall formed of billions of screens projecting billions of *spectacles*. Here, *alienation* acquires a third layer, where *false needs* take the form not of actual commodities but of representations of commodities, as aspirations, hopes, yearnings, neuroses, fantasies are sucked into a vortex of electronic *spectacles*.

6.

The Wall is a product of the Third Industrial Revolution.

Coal, steel, and steam-power were the basis of the First Industrial Revolution; the railway was the supreme symbol of the age. Oil, electricity, and motorisation were the basis of the Second Industrial Revolution; motor vehicles and consumer durables were obvious symbols. Computers, digitalisation, and instant electronic communication have been the basis of the Third Industrial Revolution; this is the age of the smartphone, tablet, and laptop.

Increasing velocity characterises each revolution. The faster goods and services can be produced, distributed, and exchanged, the quicker the money can be turned over. Money works by moving. The quicker it moves, the more it can do. The faster it turns over, the sooner it can be reinvested. The higher the velocity of money, the more rapid the accumulation of capital.

The Third Industrial Revolution has made capital in its money form weightless. It can defy the law of gravity and move faster than the speed of light. It can move from one side of the world to the other at click-button speed.

The increasing velocity of capitalism's industrial revolutions affects all aspects of social life. Before 1800, information moved at the speed of sailing ships and horse-drawn carriages. By 1875, it moved at the speed of steamships, railways, and telegraphs. By 1950, at the speed of the telephone and the radio.

But the communications technologies of the First and Second Industrial Revolutions were not bulk carriers; they could handle only small cargoes of information. To carry bulk it was necessary to digitalise and miniaturise data. This was the central technological achievement of the Third Industrial Revolution.

The Wall is a product of the digitalisation and miniaturisation of data.

The First Industrial Revolution separated human-beings from their means of production and subsistence; it imposed the *primary alienation*.

The Second Industrial Revolution, in order to sustain exponentially expanding capital accumulation, and also to sedate a growing and potentially rebellious working class, created *false needs*; this was the *second alienation*, where privatised consumption of commodities with little or no *use-value* became an opiate to compensate for loss of the collective and the creative.

The Third Industrial Revolution has transformed *false needs* for material commodities into *false needs* for virtual commodities, for electronic images, for representations and *spectacles*. This is the *third alienation*.

We can conceptualise the Wall in economic-technological terms as a product of the Third Industrial Revolution, and in social-anthropological terms as the primary expression of the *third alienation*.

Capitalism first alienated human-beings from

nature, their means of production, and their means of subsistence. It then alienated them from their real needs by substituting *false needs*. It has now alienated them from the material world of things by creating a virtual world of *spectacles*.

First we made things. Then we only consumed things. Now we merely observe things. From producer to consumer to spectator: this is the anthropological history of human *alienation* under the domination of capital.

Introduction

1.

An inpatient undergoing tests and treatment, I was taken in a wheelchair from the cancer ward on the 13th floor of University College London Hospital's tower down to the scanning department. Coming round a corner, I saw the waiting room on the right. About 15 people were sitting in chairs staring at two huge screens on the far wall. I was pushed down to the end of the front row of seats, close to the screens.

The screens, ranged side-by-side, were both showing the same image. Why two? The sound was turned up loud. A blizzard of light and sound delivering a daytime TV game show called *Bargain Hunters*. It was impossible to talk or read or think or rest. There was only the game show.

Everyone seemed to be staring blankly at the screens. I thought of the scene in Stanley Kubrick's *A Clockwork Orange* where Malcolm McDowall's eyes are pinned open in front of a cinema screen so that he can be indoctrinated. Here, in an NHS waiting room, was *the society of the spectacle* in microcosm.

2.

The inspiration for this essay was my realisation that the whole of mainstream politics has now become part of the *spectacle*. To some degree, politics has always involved *spectacle*. The burial of a pharaoh, the crowning of a king, the holding of a party rally: all *spectacles*. But an accretion of quantitative changes eventually tips into qualitative change, into a new state of being. So it is now with the politics of the system – mainstream politics, bourgeois politics, capitalist politics. Much is still said about substantive issues (though less and less); but nothing is ever done to address any of them.

Bourgeois politics has become form without

substance, performance without action, *spectacle* without meaning. It has become a façade of images where the representation has no referent, no relationship with anything concrete, material, practical. There is only spin. A kaleidoscope of *spectacles* projected onto the Wall, signifying nothing.

3.

We have entered the greatest crisis in human history. We are experiencing an ecological and social crisis, driven by exponential capital accumulation, whose end result will be the extinction of human civilisation.

Bourgeois politics has been reduced to *spectacle* because no effective action is possible in the context of exponential capital accumulation. All effective action requires negating the imperatives of capital accumulation. None can be taken without dispossessing the rich and disempowering the corporations; that is, without an international revolution of the workers, the oppressed, and the poor; without mass participatory democracy from below; without a red-green transformation based on popular power; without a restoration of *the commons*, the collective, and the creative; without a comprehensive transcendence of human *alienation*.

Piecemeal reform cannot save us. Only a new social order based on the negation of capital accumulation can do so. Therefore, bourgeois politics, embedded in the existing social order, has been reduced to a façade of *spectacles*.

4.

This essay is, in a sense, a concise theoretical history of accelerating and potentially catastrophic human *alienation*. It charts a process of *reification* in which human-beings lose control over the products of their own labour and the forces unleashed by their collective creativity. It analyses the ever-more unlimited domination of a self-feeding engine of blind, anarchic, exponential growth: the process of capital accumulation encapsulated in Marx's famous formula, $M - C - M+$, where M is the money capital originally invested, C is its transformation into energy, machinery, labour, and raw materials, and M+ is its return to the money form with an increment (surplus/profit). A process whose only purpose is to renew the cycle – forever and ever, until the end of time, until complete ecological and social breakdown and the extinction of human civilisation.

In Chapter 1, Stasis, I analyse the multi-dimensional character of the world crisis and our rapid acceleration towards comprehensive ecological and social breakdown and the extinction of human civilisation. In Chapter 2, Spectacle, I contrast this with the multi-layered *alienation* that has atomised human society, tranquillised discontent, and smothered critical thought; a pandemic of mass cognitive dissonance and stupefaction in the face of system collapse.

In Chapter 3, Creeping Fascism and Global Police State, I summarise arguments advanced elsewhere about the global shift to reaction and repression, now rehearsed in the context of the accelerating crisis of *reification* and *alienation* that is my main focus here. Chapter 4, Corporate Power and Capital Accumulation, is also a recapitulation of arguments advanced elsewhere; but arguments essential to repeat here, for the engine of the entire crisis is the process of exponential capital accumulation.

Chapters 5, 6, and 7 concern a possible alternative future: instead of accelerating ecological and social breakdown, intensifying and paralysing mass *alienation*, and rapid advance towards extinction under the rule of capital, the greatest revolutionary recasting of global society in human history. I discuss this in relation to three overarching concepts.

Chapter 5, The Commons, concerns the transcendence of the primary *alienation* – the rupture separating human-beings from nature, from one another, from the labour process and its products, from their means of production and means of subsistence, from their very *species-being*. Because humans are social animals defined by conscious, cooperative, creative labour, *the restoration of the commons* – usurped by capital – is perhaps the best description of this process.

This necessity – the existential imperative of *the restoration of the commons* if we are to prevent extinction – immediately raises the question of *revolutionary agency*. Chapter 6, The Democracy, posits the existence of a third titan of power alongside the *global police state* discussed in Chapter 3 and the corporate capital discussed in Chapter 4. I call it the *democracy*. This has nothing to do with the veneers of spin and *spectacle* to which liberal-parliamentary bourgeois democracy has been reduced. It refers to the potentially transformative power of the overwhelming majority of humanity – the workers, the oppressed, and the poor – if organised in a global movement of revolution from below and popular self-emancipation.

Chapter 7, Revolution from Below, draws the threads together and attempts to answer the old question, what is to be done, given that we must now end the rule of capital if we are to save the planet and human civilisation in the short time remaining to us.

Though many of my examples are drawn from British experience – which I know best – my theoretical generalisations concern world capitalism as a whole.

5.

This analysis does not belong to any existing Marxist tradition. It is a synthesis drawing on a wide range of traditions. As well as being influenced in my thinking by most of the classical Marxist theorists – notably, Marx, Engels, Lenin, Trotsky, and Gramsci – I have also absorbed insights from, amongst others, the economic theories of Paul Baran and Paul Sweezy, from the radical Freudian psychoanalysis of Sandor Ferenczi, Otto Rank, Wilhelm Reich, and Erich Fromm, from the Frankfurt School, especially the work of Herbert Marcuse, from the Situationist perspectives of Guy Debord, from the Fourth International tradition of Ernest Mandel, and from the International Socialist tradition of Tony Cliff.

But theory is grey and the tree of life is green. Theory is compelled to lag behind, seeking to define being when in fact there is only becoming, seeking to define what is when it has already become something else. Marxism – the theory and practice of international working-class revolution – comes closest to comprehending holistically the fluid, shape-shifting, eternally evolving nature of social reality in all its complexity, its contradictory interconnectedness, its dynamism. But Marxism cannot float through the ether; to exist it must be embodied in human practice, in the work of groups of thinkers and activists, in political organisation and the class struggle. And there it congeals into traditions and parties and sects and camps, where it forms a sediment of fossils. But in the social world, the living world, there is only motion, an eternity of change, an unstoppable torrent of becoming.

So Marxism is an unfinished research programme. Its subject matter is the past, the present, and the future, but its cutting-edge must always lie where the present is becoming the future, where contemporary theory and practice – what human-beings do – will decide the form of the future.

In this roundabout way I come to a special acknowledgement to my two closest theoretical collaborators, Phil Hearse and William I Robinson. The influence of their thinking on mine can be found on every page of this essay.

6.

Some of what follows is, therefore, an attempt at a new synthesis in which I use the 180-year-old Marxist research programme to understand the crisis of capitalism, society, and planet in the third decade of the 21st century. Relevant to this are several earlier books of my own, but in particular two studies written in collaboration with Phil Hearse and other comrades, *Creeping Fascism: what it is and how to fight it* and *System Crash: an activist guide to making revolution*. Yet more important, however, is the work of our American colleague William I Robinson, whose perspectives, developed over more than two decades, are presented in a series of seminal studies, including, most recently, *The Global Police State*. The analysis presented here builds on this foundation.

7.

I must alert readers to the dangers of a) over-abstraction and b) undialectical one-sidedness in some of the formulations in this essay. My aim is a compressed theoretical overview and a (relatively) fast read. This means stripping out caveat, nuance, qualification. This gives rise to the two dangers.

The truth is always concrete. True statements about social reality must concern the living, practical, material world as it really is. That world is a *contradictory unity in motion*. It is a collision of forces that are both bound together in a single social reality and yet at the same time are in conflict with each other. To focus on one aspect of reality is to abstract it from the *ensemble of social relations* that constitute the whole and, in a sense, to defuse it (in a theoretical sense) by disconnecting it from the other forces with which it is interacting.

One aspect of the eternal dialectical motion that constitutes social reality is that nothing that came before is ever entirely erased. Just as we bear a physical form evolved from earlier hominin species, so present-day society carries within it the reconfigured forms of past society. The third *alienation*, for example, is superimposed on the second, and the second on the first. History is a concretion of layers, ever deepening.

The text should therefore be read with two red

warning-lights switched on: beware over-abstraction and undialectical one-sidedness.

8.

A more profound reason for over-abstraction and undialectical one-sidedness is that the totality of *the contradictory unity in motion* that constitutes social reality cannot be comprehended all at once. The complexity and fluidity of the whole *ensemble of social relations* preclude cognitive grip. It is as if we wanted to catch hold of a great river.

We are compelled, therefore, to proceed by the method of extrapolation and exposition of primary tendencies; theoretically, we must identify, examine, and define these, before placing them back in their context of the whole *ensemble of social relations*, the whole *contradictory unity in motion*. Abstraction and undialectical one-sidedness are unescapable parts of the analytical process.

9.

I have adopted two unusual conventions in the text. Because the essay is a concise theoretical summation rather than an extended discourse, I have divided each chapter into a succession of numbered points of diverse character and variable length. And because the summation hinges on a series of key theoretical concepts, both vintage and newly coined, I have retained italics throughout in referencing these.

Stasis

1.

Stasis is an Ancient Greek word for which no direct English translation is possible. It means both civil strife (class struggle) and political deadlock (systemic crisis) at the same time. *Stasis* was the word used by the Ancient Greeks to describe a revolutionary situation.

Revolutionary situations can have three possible outcomes: victory for the revolutionary forces, the destruction of the *ancien regime*, and the establishment of a new political order; victory for the counter-revolutionary forces, the destruction of the popular movement, and the re-imposition of the existing order; and what Marx called 'the common ruin of the contending classes'. More prosaically, in relation to the modern world, we may speak of a choice between 'socialism and bar-barism'.

Stasis defines the current global crisis. Accel-erating ecological and social breakdown threatens the survival of human civilisation. The breakdown is propelled by the dynamo of global capital accu-mulation. Popular revolution to terminate the rule of capital is an existential imperative. Yet the rev-olutionary forces (the *democracy*) are not yet suf-ficiently organised, mobilised, equipped, and coordinated to defeat the counter-revolutionary forces (corporate capital, the *global police state*, and their reactionary and fascist allies). Therefore, the road to an alternative future is currently blocked, and we continue the slide towards oblivion.

2.

In this chapter, I focus on symptoms, not causes or cures. I seek to identify the main expressions of the global *stasis* – our current chronic condition of accelerating ecological and social crisis combined with political paralysis.

I offer the briefest summary without empirical substantiation. Fuller treatment can be found in our *System Crash*, and of course in many other studies.

3.

Climate change due to global warming is fast accelerating. All key indicators – carbon emissions, atmospheric loading, global temperatures, sea-levels, etc – are on a rising curve. Numerous signals – glacial melt, heatwaves, wildfires, droughts, storms, floods, etc – indicate that critical planetary boundaries have been breached. Climate catastrophe is already happening, with critical tipping-points now passed and irreversible changes unrolling. We have entered uncharted territory in which multiple, complex, unpredictable feed-back loops begin to transform the ecology of our planet.

The climate crisis can be understood as a *metabolic rupture* between Nature and Society – Nature in the sense of a finite but renewable resource of organic and inorganic matter capable of sustaining human life; Society in the sense of a global system of production, destruction, and waste propelled by capital accumulation.

4.

The Covid-19 pandemic constitutes another form of *metabolic rupture*. Whereas the climate crisis arises from the destruction of an existing ecology, the pandemic arises from the creation of a new ecology.

The replacement of the existing ecology by a new ecology based on the expropriation of *the commons*, the dispossession of the poor, the levelling of the wilderness, and the creation of vast monocultures has created countless global breeding-grounds for disease. The loss of biodiversity and natural firebreaks has released deadly pathogens previously trapped inside the forest. Factory farms packed with genetically identikit domesticates, slum cities filled with dispossessed people, and globalised supply-chains have created ideal conditions for the mutation and transmission of new and lethal viruses.

Covid-19 is now endemic. It will continue to evolve, giving rise to new, more transmissible, more vaccine-resistant variants. It is bleeding into a growing pandemic of Long Covid. It is squeezing capacity for other kinds of healthcare in the Global North and overwhelming all health provision across much of the Global South. It impacts disproportionately the old, the frail, the sick, the disabled, the poor, and the oppressed.

Covid-19 is still raging across the world. But corporate agribusiness has laid the foundations for an endless succession of viruses and variants. The next pandemic is only a matter of time.

5.

Climate and Covid are currently the most visceral expressions of the *metabolic rupture*. But a series of other planetary boundaries are breaking down. The nitrogen cycle, the acidity of the oceans, the loading of the environment with plastic micro-waste, the dumping of toxic pollution into land and sea, air pollution, etc: these and more are ecological crises in their own right

6.

The productive capacity of humanity – our ability to satisfy collective human need – has never been greater. This is mainly the result of the First, Second, and Third Industrial Revolutions combined with the vast expansion in world population (now 7.5 billion) consequent upon them. Technological advance has raised the productivity of labour to an unprecedented level. The labour-force available for productive work is greater than ever. Our exponentially enhanced capacity to produce *use-values* means that we are better able to provide food, clothing, shelter, comfort, education, healthcare, creative opportunity, personal fulfilment, and human self-realisation than ever before in the history of our species.

At the same time, the absolute mass of human suffering in the world has never been greater. Even

the barbarism of poverty, fascism, war, and genocide between 1929 and 1945 – which culminated
in the deaths of 60 million people – does not com-
pare with what is now unfolding. The ecological
and social crisis of the early 21st century threatens
hundreds of millions with premature death and
disablement and thousands of millions with lives
of increasing toil, destitution, disease, and misery.

This contradiction – between productive capacity and human suffering – arises from the *alienation* of humanity from nature, from society, from
the means of production and subsistence, from the
products of labour, from its own creative powers.
It arises from the usurpation of control by capital
and the subordination of productive capacity to
the imperatives of capital accumulation.

This *alienation* has given rise to unprecedented
inequality in the distribution of wealth and income. The global class structure now comprises: 1)
a tiny elite of super-rich billionaires (numbered in
the low thousands); 2) a broader elite of multi-mil-
lionaires (numbered in the low millions); 3) a large
middle class of career administrators, managers, officials, professionals, etc who serve this elite and

enjoy high material rewards (accounting for perhaps 10% of the world's population); 4) an upper mass of small-business proprietors, self-employed professionals, and skilled workers in relatively secure employment (around 30% of the total population); 5) a middle mass of workers in more casual, insecure, lower-paid 'precarious' employment (around 30%); and 6) a lower mass of destitute 'surplus humanity' more or less excluded from regular employment and attempting to survive on the margins of the economic system (around 30%). Overall, the richest 1% hold twice as much wealth as the entire world working class (groups 4, 5, and 6 combined).

The social crisis – the contradiction between human productive capacity and unsatisfied human need – is a direct consequence of global inequality in the distribution of wealth and income. This inequality is a direct consequence of an economic system based upon capital accumulation.

7.

Human needs are social needs. Britain's National Health Service can serve as a concrete example. It employs a million people. It treats a million patients every day. It exists to provide first-class medical care, free of charge, to all who need it, at the time and in the place of need. It is a masterpiece of administrative co-ordination, integrated care, and dedicated professional work designed to maximise healthcare outcomes. It is a model of cooperative labour, public service, and human solidarity.

The NHS is slowly deteriorating because the British political class, on behalf of the corporations they serve, are implementing a deliberative programme of underfunding and outsourcing designed to privatise the service. Public service is to be replaced by private profit. The result will be cost-cutting, falling standards, reduced services, increased charges, and eventually two-tier healthcare access based on ability to pay.

The slow-motion demolition of the NHS is a vivid example of the global destruction of *the commons* by advancing capital accumulation. The corporations are creating a world of private greed and public squalor.

8.

The ecological and social crisis is causing political and geopolitical breakdown. People are being dispossessed and displaced, their livelihoods destroyed; a billion people have become internal or external migrants. As economic systems and social infrastructures dissolve, political structures implode into failed states, warlordism, mafia gangs, the rule of the gun. Militarisation, violence, and war then set up new shock-waves of economic collapse and mass displacement.

Like a firestorm that grows by sucking in oxygen, the crisis becomes an accelerating vortex that feeds on the chaos of ecological, social, and political disintegration.

9.

Many wars are started deliberately. This was true of the Second World War, which was launched by the fascist regimes in Germany and Japan. Some wars arise from escalating tension, confrontation, and mission creep. The Vietnam War was of this kind: it began as a limited US intervention to prop up a client dictatorship, but evolved into a full-scale counter-insurgency war against a national independence movement. Yet other wars begin by accident; or rather, without the deliberate intent, and against the wishes, of the leading protagonists. The First World War was of this kind.

The European leaders would have avoided war in 1914 if they could have done. But they were unable to do so because Europe – a continent of warring states for hundreds of years – was too fractured by imperialist tensions, hostile alliances, vast armies, and complex war plans.

They would have been even more determined to avoid war had they known its consequences: 15 million dead, the fall of three monarchies, mass popular revulsion against existing elites and the established social order, and a tidal wave of global revolutionary struggle by workers and peasants that almost destroyed the capitalist system.

The world geopolitical system is a historically-formed patchwork of about 200 separate nation-states, ranging from global superpowers like the US and China to tiny countries of fewer than a million people. It is utterly dysfunctional. The ecological and social crisis is global and only global action can address it. Yet the framework of world capitalist politics institutionalises fragmentation, rivalry, nationalism, and militarism. This pathological geopolitical system contains an explosive charge capable of destroying everyone on the planet. A war between the major powers today – whether deliberate or accidental – could result in nuclear Armageddon.

10.

The primary expressions of humanity's greatest crisis are: climate change, pandemic disease, soaring inequality and poverty, social breakdown, escalating violence, possible nuclear annihilation.

These are the symptoms of a crisis that is driving us towards the abyss.

No aspect of the crisis is being adequately addressed. All aspects of the crisis are worsening.

The governing structures of the contemporary world order – the international institutions, summits, and conferences; the imperial states and their war-machines; the nation-states run by corrupt, pro-corporate, technocratic politicians – are unable to take effective action because they are embedded in a system based on private capital accumulation, not one based on human need and public service.

Revolution has become an existential imperative for humanity and the planet. But the popular masses are yet to achieve revolutionary agency. Therefore, at present, we continue the slide towards oblivion.

The term for this chronic condition of crisis and deadlock combined is *stasis*.

Spectacle

1.

The paralysis of bourgeois politics means that the ecological and social crisis itself has been reduced to *spectacle*. In one or another of its multiple manifestations, it is the staple fare of global news (and fake news) feeds. Heatwaves, wildfires, droughts, famines, storms, mudslides, and floods are *spectacles*. Covid infections, collapsing health services, and mass graves are *spectacles*. Mass migrations, refugee camps, militarised borders, and capsizing boats are *spectacles*. Wars, massacres, gun-toting militias in Toyota pickups, exploding buildings and streets of concrete rubble are *spectacles*.

Because the crisis only continues and intensifies, because the proclamations of bourgeois politics have no practical meaning, and because the revolutionary alternative has not yet emerged, the crisis can take only the form of *spectacle*.

2.

To recapitulate, the concept of the *spectacle* derives from the Situationist perspective of Guy Debord's *The Society of the Spectacle* (1967). I have suggested his insight represents a *third alienation*, a third layer of human estrangement from the real world.

Alienation from productive work; *alienation* from real needs; *alienation* from the material world; this threefold *alienation* gives rise to a surreal, virtual, weightless social experience. Without anchors in practical activity and material substance, mass consciousness becomes free-floating. Because nothing is tested against reality and *praxis*, anything goes, anything is possible, anything can be true.

Covid is a hoax and vaccines are toxic. Heatwaves and floods are fake news. Islam is a conspiracy. Migrants are a threat. Jeremy Corbyn is a racist. Donald Trump is a genius. Boris Johnson loves the NHS.

Discourse is no longer communication about an actually existing world; it is an eternal shaking of a lucky-dip of soundbites, tweets, memes, and hashtags; an endless churning of data molecules without connection or context.

Increasingly, too, images replace discourse. Unmediated sensory experience then substitutes for any kind of thought, even the crudest, let alone scientific thought, rational thought, critical thought.

3.

Anything and everything can become *spectacle*. An infinite variety of images can be created with click-button speed. Images can be sent across the world in seconds. Billions of people act as transmitters. Billions of screens act as receivers.

The Roman ruling class used 'bread and circuses' to placate the Roman mob. The modern ruling class offers an endless succession of electronic *spectacles* – sporting championships, state ceremonies, celebrity weddings, commemorative events, international summits, music festivals, etc. They offer an ever-expanding range of instant-access, personally-selected, zero-effort electronic entertainment. They supply a constant drip-feed of electronic hoardings for every conceivable kind of consumer pap. They prey on neurotic unease, on low self-esteem, on the inner hollowness of alienated humanity. Frustrated aspirations – to be rich, beautiful, fashionable, elegant, sexy, clever, respected, successful, whatever – discover a catalogue of commodities to satisfy them.

Social media is also spectacular. Narcissistic self-exposures firecracker across the internet. Cereal-packet trivia clicks its way across cyberspace. FOMO-anxious addicts check their feeds, add their comments, make their shares – every hour, every ten minutes, every spare moment. Corporate algorithms read each click in a second and trigger a customised tweak to the individual user's flow of marketing, fake news, celebrity tittle-tattle, and other bullshit.

The internet becomes an immaterial world of virtual lives constructed of electronic bric-a-brac; a world of totally immersive *alienation* where nothing is done, nothing is made, where no real human relations are formed, no practical action performed, where *species-being* reduces to zero.

4.

Species-being is libidinal. *Alienation* is psychic rupture. Defined as a species by cooperative creative labour, our minds are hard-wired for connection with others, solidarity with others, union with others. The *society of the spectacle*, the *third alienation*, is therefore a form of mass psychosis. It means that *libido* – the psychic life-force – is no longer projected outwards to lovers, family, friends, colleagues, creative work, the public good, society as a whole – but is inverted into *extreme narcissistic individualism*.

The atomisation of society into individual workers, consumers, and spectators, the disintegration of civil society, especially of organisations of collective struggle like the unions, creates a psychic dystopia, a rupture of *species-being* at the most intimate level of basic libidinal health. It is characterised by what Fromm called 'fear of freedom' – a chronic, debilitating lack of confidence, independence, willpower, and creativity. It involves an inversion of deformed, misdirected *libido*, a lack of fulfilment and aspiration, a festering psychic misery liable to explosions of psychotic rage.

5.

The society of the *spectacle* is also a politics of the *spectacle*. Bourgeois politics comprises an endless sequence of displays – global summits, world conferences, meetings of state leaders, official visits, party conferences, parliamentary debates. International institutions – the United Nations, the World Economic Forum, the EU, NATO, many others – organise *spectacles*. National political institutions do the same. Each event is heralded with great fanfare, loaded with import, discussed gravely. Commentators describe the players, the body language, the nuances. They dissect the speeches and statements. Platitudes become wisdom. Vacuity becomes statesmanship. Nothingness becomes a historical event.

Take the annual COP conferences (United Nations Climate Change Conferences) held since

1995. The purpose of these international gatherings of thousands of politicians, scientists, and lobbyists is to agree, coordinate, and implement a global response to climate change. The fate of the planet is imagined to hinge on the outcome. But COP is only a *spectacle*. The accelerating gravity of the crisis, and the measures necessary to resolve it, are explained. Then targets are set and pledges made that bear no relation to the measures necessary. Then these targets and pledges are forgotten anyway. COP turns out to have been nothing more than political showbiz.

The world has been getting hotter, and faster, for 25 years. Since the first COP conference, increases in carbon emissions, atmospheric loading, global temperatures, and sea-levels have continued to accelerate. COP has made no difference.

Take another example: the bourgeois political response to the Covid-19 pandemic. This ranges from the fascist-eugenicist policies of far-right regimes like that of Johnson in Britain to the attempted containment policies of more liberal regimes like that of Biden in the US. But, in the context of a global health emergency, the main-

stream political system is incapable of implementing a comprehensive programme of appropriate
action. Nor does the official 'opposition' even raise
the most basic and obvious reformist demands. In
Britain, for instance, those demands might include: huge public investment in expanded healthcare capacity; a big pay rise for NHS staff and a
massive recruitment and training programme to
fill vacancies; immediate termination of all outsourcing and privatisation in the NHS; abolition
of patents, nationalisation of Big Pharma, and
huge public investment in vaccine production and
roll-out for the Global South. The Labour Party
could champion these demands. The trade unions
could fight for them. But they are not even
mooted. The dominance of neoliberal ideology,
rooted in the imperatives of global capital accumulation, precludes a rational collective response to
the pandemic. The age of reason and progress is
over. We live in an age of madness.

Even the opposition has become part of the
spectacle. Social-democratic and liberal parties,
once standard-bearers of progressive reform, are
run by career technocrats representing the rich and

the corporations; their 'opposition' is façade. Trade unions, once the combat organisations of working-class struggle, have become bureaucracies of lobbyists. Campaign groups organise token marches, protests, and stunts, but they rarely transition from protest to resistance – from mere expression of dissent to class struggle capable of challenging the power of capital and the state.

Limited protest can be tolerated because it is part of the *spectacle*: momentary, regulated, ineffective, it is part of the façade of liberal-parliamentary democracy which masks the substantive reality of corporate power, capital accumulation, and the *global police state*.

Protest is not struggle. Struggle is an open clash of class forces, a direct pitting of the collective power of workers, the oppressed, and the poor against the repressive power of capital and the state. Strikes, pickets, occupations, blockades, etc – anything that challenges the power of capital and the state – is constrained by bourgeois law and police repression. So real struggle invariably involves mass law-breaking and confrontations with the police. Class struggle looks like the miners strike of

1984-85 or the poll tax revolt of 1989-91. It strips away the liberal veneer of the state to expose its repressive essence. When capital is threatened by struggle from below, the state is revealed as 'armed bodies of men and women' (Engels).

6.

Bourgeois politics is now part of the society of the *spectacle*. Unable to address effectively any aspect of the accelerating ecological and social crisis – because that crisis is rooted in the imperatives of world capital accumulation and therefore cannot be resolved without international revolution and a red-green transition powered by popular mass mobilisation from below – all kinds of bourgeois politics, including formalised dissent and 'opposition', become form without content, façade without substance, a succession of *spectacles*.

Mainstream politics, official politics, despite all the pomp and circumstance, is just another part of the Wall. It is wholly encompassed within the *third alienation*. It reflects humanity's loss of control over the material world that is both its natural substrate and its active creation.

Creeping Fascism and Global Police State

1.

Fascism is the hyper-charging of a nexus of traditional reactionary ideas – authoritarianism, militarism, nationalism, racism, sexism, homophobia, etc – to create an active counter-revolutionary political bloc. It provides capital and the state with a mass electoral base and a mass street force, including, when necessary, armed militia, in the context of deep and intractable social crisis.

2.

Fascism is a process. It develops in relation to the crisis and in collision with other social forces. Before the outbreak of the Second World War, six years after Hitler came to power, there were only about 25,000 people in Nazi concentration camps, and only a few hundred people had been killed by Nazi paramilitaries. The conquest of Poland (1939) and then Western Russia (1941) created the context for the Holocaust. Only in 1941 did the Nazis commence large-scale mass murder, and only in 1944 did this reach a peak with industrialised genocide in purpose-built extermination camps. They eventually murdered about 20 million. Fascism must be understood as a tendency, not a *fait accompli*.

3.

The existing bourgeois state apparatus is always the primary instrument of fascist repression and totalitarianism. The state is reconfigured by a process of *gleichschaltung* ('coordination') – achieved by a mix of purge, intimidation, and indoctrination – and thus brought into line with fascist ideology and programme. Fascist paramilitaries are always auxiliaries.

4.

Fascism takes many different concrete forms. The Italian Fascists took several years to complete the process of *gleichschaltung* and create a totalitarian state; they never organised a systematic genocide. The Spanish Falangists remained a subordinate part of a counter-revolutionary alliance led by army generals during the Spanish Civil War; they supplied military contingents and death-squads. The Japanese Militarists had their origins as a movement of army officers; they transformed the existing army into the primary mechanism for creating a totalitarian state.

5.

Second-wave fascism – what we have called *creeping fascism* – is different from first-wave interwar fascism. Two differences are especially significant.

First, the absence of a mass, organised, militant working-class movement means that fascist paramilitaries and street-fighting are less necessary; the primary role of the existing bourgeois state in the development of fascism is even more pronounced.

Second, the exceptional atomisation and *alienation* characteristic of neoliberal capitalism mean that the blood-and-soil nationalism, imagined communities, invented traditions, etc of interwar fascism – where the individual is subordinate to and subsumed within the mass – is no longer dominant. Instead, *creeping fascism* is underpinned by *extreme narcissistic individualism*. The culture war is essentially an ideological struggle between the solidarity and humanity represented by the progressive working class and the nihilistic selfishness of a proto-fascist reactionary bloc formed of the petty-bourgeoisie and a 'lumpenised' reactionary working class.

6.

In interwar fascism, the leader represented the authoritarian father-figure of the traditional patriarchal bourgeois family. The 'little man' (Reich's term), in flight from freedom, seems to have found relief from guilt, anxiety, and insecurity through immersion in the mass, in a swallowing up of person in the movement and the nation, in obedience to the all-knowing, all-powerful, God-like leader.

The mass psychology of second-wave fascism is differently configured. Instead of libido dissolving into a mythic national community, it is inverted, turns in on itself, becoming an extreme, selfish, narcissistic individualism. The leader is no longer an authoritarian father-figure, but a mirror in which the hyper-alienated, socio-pathic, self-obsessed consumer-spectators of an atomised social order see themselves.

7.

Creeping fascism creates an ideological and political mass base for capital and the state in a period of acute and accelerating crisis in which reform and improvement are precluded. But the system cannot hope to achieve general consent. The material reality of deteriorating social conditions, of increasing exploitation, oppression, and poverty, means explosions of popular rage against the system. This in turn means more militarised and violent police repression. William I Robinson uses the concept of the *global police state* to analyse this development.

8.

Global police state does not mean that there is a single, centralised, pan-global police authority. It means that each nation-state deploys police to safeguard the interests of *transnational capital* within its own national territory – much as individual police departments operate in separate localities inside each nation-state.

9.

In addition to crushing mass resistance to the rule of capital and the state when necessary, the *global police state* has also become a primary form of modern capital accumulation.

During the Cold War, the permanent arms economy involved high levels of state arms expenditure, lucrative contracts for arms manufacturers, and a multiplier-effect stimulus to the wider economy; the military-industrial complex was one of the engines of post-war capitalism.

Today, in addition to continuation of the permanent arms economy in the context of the War on Terror, there is unprecedented expenditure on militarised policing, border controls, detention-centres, mass surveillance, etc. *Militarised accumulation* – state spending on armed forces, police, and repression – is an engine of neoliberal capitalism.

10.

The Wall – the society and the politics of the *spectacle* as transmitted through cyberspace to ten billion screens – is capital's first line of defence. The Wall combines mind-numbing pap, consumerism, and reactionary ideology. It is the primary mechanism for achieving consent, indifference, apathy, passivity, etc in the context of escalating ecological and social crisis.

But as the crisis deepens, the system is threatened by spontaneous explosions of popular revolt from below. *Creeping fascism* divides the working class and provides capital and the state with a mass political base and auxiliary street forces in the face of popular revolt. The *global police state* provides the concentrated, militarised, repressive power to smash such revolt.

The existing bourgeois state apparatus is both the primary agent of *creeping fascism* and the local franchise of the *global police state*. Mass surveillance, repressive laws, militarised police, and nationalist-racist ideology herald a new *totalitarianism*.

6

Corporate Power and Capital Accumulation

1.

Capital can be defined as the self-expansion of value – in Marx's formula, $M - C - M+$, where M is the money capital originally invested, C is the conversion of this money capital into plant, labour, and raw materials during the production process, and $M+$ is the return to the money form when commodities are sold, but with added value (surplus/profit).

Without profit, there is no incentive to invest and there is economic stagnation and mass unemployment. The world capitalist economy expands at the rate of approximately 3% per annum; this means it doubles in size every quarter of a century. Capitalism is a system of exponential growth without end.

2.

Capitalism is a highly contradictory economic system. It is characterised by a long-term tendency towards *over-accumulation* and *under-consumption*.

Workers are paid less than the value of their labour; if this were not the case, there would be no profit. This means the working class as a whole cannot consume the entire output of its labour, because the aggregate value of wages is always lower than the aggregate value of the commodities produced. The system therefore has a built-in tendency to become overloaded with surplus capital.

3.

The long-term tendency towards *over-accumulation* and *under-consumption* has become more severe with the development of monopoly-capitalism, where each sector of the economy is dominated by a small number of giant firms able to collude to reduce competition, manage markets, create demand, fix prices, and increase profits. The effect is to further overload the system with surplus capital.

It was monopoly-capitalism that created the consumer society based on *false needs* critiqued by Herbert Marcuse in *One-Dimensional Man* (amongst others). Seminal theorists of monopoly-capitalism – and of the growing tendency towards stagnation due to *over-accumulation* and *under-consumption* – were Paul Baran and Paul Sweezy, notably in *The Theory of Capitalist Development* (1942) and *Monopoly Capital: an essay on the American economic and social order* (1966). The work of Baran and Sweezy has provided the foundation for further work by John Bellamy Foster and other theorists associated with *Monthly Review*.

4.

From the late 19th to the late 20th century, world capitalism was dominated by giant multinational/imperialist corporations. The handful of corporations dominant in each sector tended to retain a primary national base where most production was concentrated, but they sought raw materials and markets on a global scale. This explains the murderous imperialist wars – essentially attempts by rival great powers to redivide the world in the interests of their own capitalists – of the early 20th century (the First and Second World Wars), and also the nuclear-armed confrontation and local proxy wars of the late 20th century (the Cold War).

But – as William I Robinson has explained in *A Theory of Global Capitalism* (2004), *Global Capitalism and the Crisis of Humanity* (2014), and other works – the neoliberal era (c.1975-present) has seen a shift from multinational to *transnational capital*. Whereas multinational capital remains anchored in a primary national base, *transnational capital*, irrespective of where a corporation is headquartered/registered, is characterised by fully globalised production, distribution, and marketing. *Transnational capital* is now the hegemonic fraction of global capital, dwarfing the operations of national, regional, and local capitals.

The transnational giants are often *hollow corporations*. This is especially true of finance and tech giants. These are dominant by virtue of control over money capital and/or marketing networks. They produce nothing – all production is outsourced – but they cream off the bulk of the profit.

The dominance of *transnational capital* and the emergence of *hollow corporations* are in large part a consequence of the Third Industrial Revolution based on digitalised-electronic data capture, storage, and processing, and on instant online global communications.

5.

Throughout its existence, capitalism has been compelled to find ways to resolve its intrinsic crisis of *over-accumulation* by offloading surplus capital. Because the crisis of *over-accumulation* has intensified over time, this process has become increasingly pathological. It has reached a new peak in the neoliberal era. It is the underlying and deepening crisis of *over-accumulation* that explains all the following characteristics of contemporary capitalism: financialisation, rising exploitation at the point of consumption, hyper-consumerism, the privatisation of *the commons*, and state-funded accumulation.

6.

Financialisation is accumulation through the creation and investment of fictitious money capital. Governments and banks create money by entering numbers in computers. This money can then be invested in financial assets. These assets return a profit either in the form of interest or because they have attained higher value when sold on.

Money is a form of debt. Financialisation is anchored in rising levels of debt – public, corporate, and household – typically with real estate as the foundation, especially mortgages. But this anchorage is insecure.

Mountains of fictitious capital are created. Financial asset values tend to rise because of the continuing flow of new electronic money into the system, and trading can sometimes become frenzied, with exponentially rising values, speculative bubbles, and banking crashes.

Nothing is produced. Financialisation means profiting without producing. It is pure parasitism. If the formula for industrial accumulation is M – C – M+, that for financial accumulation is M – (M) – M+, where M is the money capital originally invested, (M) is the financial asset purchased, and M+ is the increased money capital realised through interest payments or rising asset values.

Debt-based financialisation – the 'permanent debt economy' – has absorbed a huge and rising mass of surplus capital in the neoliberal era.

7.

The working class is exploited as workers at the point of production (where it is paid less than the value of its labour) and as consumers at the point of consumption (in the form of fees, rents, high prices, interest on debt, state taxes, etc). The neoliberal era has seen a relative shift to higher rates of exploitation, and therefore surplus accumulation, at the point of consumption.

This shift has been underpinned by rising levels of debt. Working-class households are now saddled with unprecedented amounts of debt. Both the debt itself and the higher levels of consumption it enables are sources of profit.

8.

The consumer society powered by *false needs* has been hyper-charged under neoliberalism. Debt enables high levels of consumer spending despite falling or stagnant wages. The sales effort (branding, packaging, advertising, etc) now takes the primary form of customised online *spectacle* mediated by corporate algorithms. Atomisation and *alienation* stimulate neurotic consumerism. The spiritual emptiness of everyday life, the psychic misery of modern humanity, creates a mass market for every species of corporate snake-oil merchant.

9.

The remaining *commons* – social housing, public healthcare, major utilities, public transport, local services, etc – are being sold off to private capital.

Services previously provided collectively, at public expense, by government agencies, are contracted out to private corporations. In effect, state taxes, instead of funding not-for-profit public services are used to fund private capital accumulation – a direct transfer from working-class incomes (levied as taxes) to corporate profit.

10.

In the mid 20th century, the state played a proactive role in economic management, with high levels of public provision, nationalisation, regulation, etc. In the early 21st century, the role of the state is to service *transnational capital*.

As well as crushing resistance from below as the local franchise of the *global police state*, the modern nation-state apparatus provides contracts, subsidies, and bailouts to private capital, recycling tax revenues and state debt into corporate profit.

This takes many forms. *Militarised accumulation* – rising expenditure on armaments, police, prisons, security, borders, spying, etc – is one. State bailouts of bankrupt banks when speculative bubbles burst is another. Contracting private health corporations to provide NHS services is another. There are many more.

11.

Modern capitalism can be defined as a system of globalised, financialised, monopoly-capitalism, dominated by *transnational* mega-corporations, afflicted with a chronic and deepening crisis of *over-accumulation* and *under-consumption*, increasingly prone to stagnation and slump, and increasingly pathological and parasitic in its efforts to unload surplus capital.

Nonetheless, the neoliberal mix of financialisation, permanent debt, manic consumption, privatisation, and state-funded accumulation sustains ongoing global capital accumulation even in the face of accelerating ecological and social breakdown.

The future – under the rule of capital and the *global police state* – can be expressed in a simple formula, $(M - C - M+)\infty = X$, where $(M - C - M+)$ is capital accumulation, ∞ is infinity, and X is extinction. Because capital is, by definition, the self-expansion of value, exponential growth without limit until the end of time, it now constitutes an existential threat to human civilisation.

The second part of this essay considers the alternative: international revolution from below to create real democracy, restore *the commons*, and effect a red-green transition to an egalitarian social order and an ecological sustainable economy.

The Commons

1.

The history of the class struggle for 5,000 years has been the history of the struggle between private property and *the commons*.

In pre-class society, nature, the land, the means of production, etc had been utilised collectively. Only with the development of class society – in which a few who did not work lived off the labour of the many who did – was it necessary to create forms of private property.

The forms have varied. Property might be held by an elite collectively. Ancient temple priesthoods, the medieval church hierarchy, the multiple shareholders of a big corporation, and modern party-state bureaucracies are all examples. Or it might be held by a single owner or family. But the principle is the same: private property is the usurpation of *the commons* by a ruling class.

2.

Only now is the long class war between private property and *the commons* reaching completion.

In the medieval period, some peasants still owned their own land, many had customary tenancies hedged with legal protections, and all enjoyed a range of common rights, like free access to the woods to collect firewood or pasture pigs. Most peasants had their own plots, their own tools, and provided much of their own subsistence, even if they had obligations to their lords to perform labour-service and pay rents, tithes, and taxes. Manorial court records are full of disputes which revolve around the respective (private) rights of the lords and (common) rights of the peasants.

Capitalism involves the displacement of the peasantry from the land, its dispossession of its own means of production and subsistence, and its conversion into a working class without property or common rights, and therefore with nothing to sell but its labour-power.

It is this process – part of the wider 500-year process of capitalist globalisation – that is now reaching its completion with the slow destruction of the residual peasantry in the Global South.

3.

Though the long-term trajectory is towards destruction of *the commons* by the ruling class, the curve is uneven. Upsurges in class struggle from below can interrupt, even reverse, the process.

During 'the trade-union century' (late 19th to late 20th century), the working class was strong enough to win major social reforms and thereby expand the terrain of *the commons*. The welfare states of this period involved subsidised social housing, controlled rents, free education, free healthcare, and much more – an expanded realm of collective provision at public expense.

But the world crisis of the 1970s and the neoliberal counter-revolution of the 1980s brought this period to an end.

4.

The power of the trade unions (and of the reformist social-democratic political tradition based upon them) was broken during the 1980s. Over the last 40 years, workplace trade unionism, rooted social-democratic politics, and working-class community more generally, have largely disintegrated; the working class has ceased to be an organised collective force; society has been atomised, reduced to its smallest units, the individual worker, consumer, spectator.

Token protest has replaced class struggle. It may be planned – like the Occupy and Extinction Rebellion movements – or it may be more spontaneous – like the Black Lives Matter and Palestine Solidarity demonstrations. But the protests rise like a rocket only to fall like a stick. The dog barks but the caravan moves on. There is much noise, but capital and the state are not threatened, policy does not change, and the protests turn out to have been merely another kind *spectacle*.

5.

The destruction of *the commons* therefore continues apace. The dissonance between thought and action, rhetoric and policy, *spectacle* and substance has never been greater. The Tories clap for the NHS while pushing forward its privatisation. They proclaim outrage at racist abuse of football players while militarising the border against African migrants. They condemn male against violence women but order a police attack on a vigil for a murdered woman. They host a climate-change conference but continue expanding fossil-fuel capacity, subsidising carbon polluters, building new roads, and ripping up environmental protections.

The dissonance extends to dissidents and protestors. Most are merely lobbyists who 'call on' the political representatives of capital and the state to halt privatisation, eradicate poverty, take action against racism, end male violence, stop global warming, etc. They 'call on' the ruling class to halt the destruction of *the commons* by global capital accumulation – much as one might have 'called on' slaveowners to abolish slavery or feudal lords to abolish feudalism.

6.

Capitalism is the most rapacious, relentless, all-consuming social system in human history. Previous social systems were geographically localised and slow to develop. Capitalism is a dynamic system of global reach and exponential growth, eternally restless, eternally pushing towards, and finally beyond, what is ecologically and socially sustainable.

After 5,000 years of class society, and especially after 500 years of capitalist class society, the usurpation of *the commons* by private property now threatens the very survival of human civilisation. The restoration of *the commons* has become an existential imperative. This can be achieved only by the overthrow of the *global police state*, the dispossession of the rich, the halting of capital accumulation, and the creation of a new democratic order. It can be achieved only by the ending of human *alienation*. It can be achieved only by an international revolution of the working class, the oppressed, and the poor.

7.

The alternative – the unalienated world of *the commons* – exists in microcosm everywhere. On an NHS hospital ward, integrated teams of doctors, nurses, allied professionals, and ancillary staff engage in skilled, cooperative, practical work devoted to human welfare. That work is poisoned by the miasma of capital – it occurs in a context of underfunding, privatisation, staff shortages, stagnant/falling wages, excessive hours, and management bullying. The contradiction between the unalienated world of *the commons* and the alienated world of capital accumulation is a lived daily experience in public service. But here we glimpse a possible alternative future.

The Democracy

1.

Democracy, like *stasis*, is an Ancient Greek word. The *demos* – in contrast to the *aristoi* (nobles) or *oligoi* (the few) – was the majority fraction of the citizen-body of the *polis* (city-state), mainly farmers but also craftworkers, petty traders, and other working people. The *demos* did not include women, children, slaves, and foreigners. Only free-born adult male citizens had political rights. But this gives the word a special meaning: the *demos* was the citizen-body organised as a political force.

The history of the Greek city-states is the history of the class struggle between the many (*demos*) and the few (*oligoi*). Greek democracy was the active, direct, participatory democracy of the sovereign *demos*. Modern liberal-parliamentary democracy, by contrast, is a façade of *spectacles* masking the power of capital and the state, where the masses are passive election fodder.

The term *democracy* is here used in the Ancient Greek sense. It implies an organised, mobilised, self-acting social force.

2.

Reappropriation of the term *democracy* is necessary.

The entire reformist tradition hinges on the idea of representation: workers are not expected to exercise power directly, but to elect politicians to represent their interests and carry out reforms, in the framework of liberal-parliamentary democracy, that is, in the framework of the bourgeois state. Social-democratic politics is thereby incorporated into the system and becomes a mechanism for channelling and containing the class struggle. It is a pressure-value to protect the system.

The entire Stalinist tradition also hinges on the idea of representation. In this case, however, a

party-state bureaucracy (and its repressive apparatus) is imagined to represent the interests of the
working class. The absurd notion that a totalitarian dictatorship, complete with censorship, secret
police, violent suppression of dissent, a network
of prison camps, a massive war machine, etc, can
somehow represent the interests of the working
class has been shockingly tenacious for almost a
century, ever since the destruction of the last ves-
tiges of the Russian revolutionary movement by
Stalinist counter-revolution in the winter of 1927/
8. This notion evolved into 'campism' when the
Stalinist monolith broke up, with different Stalinist states – Russia, Yugoslavia, China, Albania, etc
– at loggerheads. We ended up with pro-Russian,
pro-Chinese, pro-Cuban, even pro-Albanian, etc
political sects.

One consequence has been intractable seman-
tic confusion. Terms like socialism and commu-
nism have lost clarity because of their
appropriation by Stalinism. That is not to say that
democracy is not also a tainted term. But it has this
virtue. It reasserts the living essence of the revolutionary Marxist tradition. It underlines that the

emancipation of the working class is the act of the working class – not the act of reformist politicians, or party bureaucrats, or tanks with red stars – and that the necessary organisational form of such self-emancipation is mass, participatory, democratic assemblies.

3.

The first great experiment in mass participatory working-class democracy was the Paris Commune of March-May 1871. The Communards smashed the old state apparatus in the city of Paris and created a new bottom-up state rooted in democratic assemblies in each suburb. Though it was crushed by counter-revolution after two months, Marx proclaimed the Commune to have been 'the political form at last discovered under which to work out the political emancipation of labour'. As he explained in *The Civil War in France* (1871):

The working class cannot simply lay hold of the ready-made state machinery and wield it for its own purposes ...

The first decree of the Commune was ... the suppression of the standing army and the substitution for it of the armed people.

The Commune was formed of the municipal councillors, chosen by universal suffrage in the various wards of the town, responsible and revocable at short terms. The majority of its members were naturally working men, or acknowledged representatives of the working class. The Commune was to be a working, not a parliamentary body, executive and legislative at the same time.

Instead of continuing to be the agent of the central government, the police was at once stripped of its political attributes and turned into the at all times revocable agent of the Commune. So were the officials of all other branches of the administration.

From the members of the Commune downwards, the public service had to be done at workmen's wages. The vested interests and the representation allowances of the high dignitaries of state disappeared along with the high dignitaries themselves.

Public functions ceased to be the private property of the tools of the central government. Not only municipal administration, but the whole initiative hitherto exercised by the state was laid into the hands of the Commune.

Having once got rid of the standing army and the police, the physical force elements of the old government, the Commune was anxious to break the spiritual force of repression, the 'parson-power', by the disestablishment and disendowment of all churches as proprietary bodies. The priests were sent back to the recesses of private life ...

The whole of the educational institutions were opened to the people free of charge, and at the same time cleared of all interference by church and state...

The judicial functionaries were to be divested of that sham independence which had but served to mask their abject subservience to all successive governments ... Like the rest of public servants, magistrates and judges were to be elective, responsible, and revocable ...

The Commune constitution would have restored to the social body all the forces hitherto absorbed by the state parasite feeding upon, and clogging up, the free movement of society ... the Commune ... was a thoroughly expansive political form, while all previous forms of government had been emphatically repressive. Its true secret was this: it was essentially a working-class government, the product of the struggle of the producing against the appropriating class, the political form at last discovered under which to work out the economic emancipation of labour.

4.

History has proved Marx right. Again and again in the 150 years since the Commune, whenever the working class, the oppressed, and the poor have risen in revolutionary struggle, they have been compelled to create organs of mass participatory democracy to drive the struggle forwards.

In the Russian Revolutions of 1905 and 1917, the soviets – democratic assemblies of workers, soldiers, sailors, and peasants – sent their delegates to the Petrograd Soviet, and this became the main organising centre of the entire revolution. It was the concentrated expression of the democratic will of hundreds of thousands of people in the capital city. In Trotsky's words:

The soviets are the most perfect representatives of the people – perfect in their revolutionary experience, in their ideas and objects. Based directly upon the army in the trenches, the workers in the factories, and the peasants in the fields, they are the backbone of the revolution.

The soviets were the means by which the most downtrodden and marginalised in society – 'the Dark People' – were drawn into political activity and became a political force for the first time. Describing the mass meetings of the soviets held across Petrograd on the eve of the October Revolution, Trotsky wrote:

The people of the slums, of the attics and basements, stood still by the hour in threadbare coat or grey uniform, with caps or heavy shawls on their heads, the mud of the streets soaked through their shoes, an autumn cough catching at their throats. They stood there packed shoulder-to-shoulder, and crowding even closer to make room for more, to make room for all, listening tirelessly, hungrily, passionately, demandingly, fearing lest they miss a word of what it is so necessary to understand, to assimilate, and to do ...

5.

In Barcelona in 1936, the revolutionary committees played a similar role – a mesh of mainly anarchist-dominated committees that had sprung up in July to run collectivised farms, worker-controlled factories, rural villages, city suburbs, and the militias formed to fight the fascist counter-revolution. George Orwell, an eyewitness who joined one of the militias, described the character of revolutionary Barcelona thus:

It was the first time I had ever been in a town where the working class was in the saddle. Practically every building of any size had been seized by the workers and was draped with red flags or with the red and black flag of the anarchists; every wall was scrawled with the hammer and the sickle and with the initials of the revolutionary parties; almost every church had been gutted and its images burnt. Churches here and there were being systematically demolished by gangs of workmen. Every shop and café had its inscription saying it had been collectivised; even the bootblacks had been collectivised and their boxes painted red and black...

There were no private motor-cars, they had all been commandeered, and all the trams and taxis and much of the other transport were painted red and black. The revolutionary posters were everywhere, flaming from the walls in clean reds and blues that made the few remaining advertisements look like daubs of mud. Down the Ramblas, the wide central artery of the town where crowds of people streamed constantly to and fro, the loudspeakers were bellowing revolutionary songs all day and far into the night.

And it was the aspect of the crowds that was the queerest thing of all. In outward appearance it was a town in which the wealthy classes had practically ceased to exist ... Practically everyone wore rough working-class clothes, or blue overalls, or some variant of the militia uniform.

All this was queer and moving. There was much in it that I did not understand, in some ways I did not even like it, but I recognised it immediately as a state of affairs worth fighting for.

6.

On 14 November 1956, in response to a Russian invasion by 200,000 troops and 3,000 tanks to suppress a popular movement, the workers of Budapest formed a soviet, the Central Workers' Council of Greater Budapest. On the 21 November, it issued an appeal to the Hungarian working class as a whole, which stated:

The Central Workers' Council, democratically elected by the Budapest industries and districts, turns to you with information and an appeal in order that we might make our ranks stronger and more united.

As you know, the Central Workers' Council of

Greater Budapest was created on 14 November on the initiative of the large industries in order to co-ordinate the work of the workers' councils in the factories and represent our common demands ...

The factories are in our hands, the hands of the workers' councils, but to increase our strength further and to make possible a common stand on behalf of common measures, we hold the following tasks to be the most important:

- *In every district and county where district or county workers' councils have not yet been created, such organs should immediately be elected democratically from below. To this end, large industries – particularly those in county seats – should initiate the creation of central councils.*
- *Each district and county central council should immediately establish contact with the Central Workers' Council of Greater Budapest ...*
- *One of the most important tasks of the factory workers' councils, apart from the organisation*

of work, is the urgent election of permanent workers' councils ...

- *Furthermore, it is very important that the elections of the new factory committees should be taken in hand by the representatives of the genuine will of the working class, the workers' councils ...*
- *The district and county workers' councils should at once establish contact with the distribution centre of the Red Cross and should send their representatives to headquarters to ensure just distribution on a social basis ...*
- *The district and county workers' councils should appoint social control organs to keep an eye on prices in the markets and shops. Social inspectors should regularly visit sales premises and report possible abuses to the proper authorities, after exposing the perpetrator to public contempt.*
- *The district and county councils should make every effort to keep public opinion informed; if there is an opportunity, they should demand space in the local press and constantly inform*

*the workers of the factories and other indus-
trial premises of the true situation ...*

7.

In June 1973, in response to an attempted military
coup against the left-reformist government of Sal-
vador Allende in Chile, a communiqué was issued
by the *Cordon* Cerrillos in Greater Santiago. The
cordones constituted a fast-growing network of local soviets, with *comandos comunales* as their joint
organising committees. The Cerrillos communiqué was an appeal to this movement setting out
immediate tasks in response to the coup attempt:

- *Take over all factories.*
- *Organise brigades of 11 comrades, with one
  leader; the leaders of each brigade, together
  with the trade-union organisers, will take over
  the organisation of the factory.*
- *Centralise within the factory all vehicles and
  materials that may be useful for the defence*

of the factory, the working class, and the government.

- *Every hour on the hour each factory should sound its siren to indicate that all is well. If help is needed, the siren should be sounded continuously.*
- *Keep permanently tuned to Radio Corporation.*
- *Place a guard on the most visible point in the factory.*
- *Maintain constant communication with surrounding factories and appoint comrades to act as couriers.*
- *Say where the* commando *will be located and where leading comrades will meet if access is impossible.*
- *Organise assemblies and keep the workers informed.*

8.

Further examples could be cited. An embryonic network of popular assemblies and workers' commissions developed during the Portuguese Revolution of 1974-75. The *shoras* of the Iranian Revolution of 1979 often exerted full control over the workplaces, operated independently of official managers and the state, and based themselves on the interests of rank-and-file workers. Around 10 million workers – 80% of the total workforce – joined the insurrectionary trade union Solidarność (Solidarity) during the Polish social crisis of 1980-81.

But less advanced forms of class struggle also involve mass democratic organisation. In August 1969, in response to violent sectarian attacks by Protestant police and mobs, the Catholic-Nationalist population of Derry in the North of Ireland, mainly concentrated in the Bogside and Creggan estates, mounted a full-scale urban uprising ('the Battle of the Bogside') which established an extensive 'no-go' area under local control which endured for three years.

Mass struggles by British workers against the

Tory Government of Edward Heath between 1970 and 1974 defeated a programme of wage cuts and union-busting. These struggles involved strikes, mass pickets, open defiance of the law, and violent clashes with the police. Central to the movement was a nationwide network of shop-stewards (elected workplace representatives) and workplace mass meetings where decisions were made by show of hands.

The 1984-5 British miners' strike was organised by the National Union of Mineworkers (NUM). Each colliery had its own NUM lodge (branch). The lodge leadership was directly elected and regular mass meetings of the entire lodge membership were held throughout the year-long strike.

The 1989-91 poll tax revolt was organised by local anti-poll tax unions (ATPUs). Set up by activists on local estates, the ATPUs were open to all local residents who joined the tax strike.

Countless other examples of democratic organisation in the context of mass struggle could be cited. The central lesson of the historical experience is that revolutionary and other mass class struggles necessarily give rise to organs of democracy from below.

9.

Marx had grasped the world-shaking historical significance of the Paris Commune in 1871. He said the Communards had 'stormed the heavens'. Numerous historical examples since have proved him right.

In some cases, the masses have carried out a socialist revolution, smashed the old state apparatus, and established a short period of popular democratic rule – for two months in Paris in 1871, for a few years in Russia after 1917, for a year or so in Barcelona in 1936-37. In most cases, for various complex reasons, they have failed to achieve even this. Why this history of failure?

Social forces of immense wealth, power, and influence stand opposed to the popular movement. Even when a limited breakthrough occurs, it can usually be sealed off and destroyed by economic sanctions and military aggression. Capitalism is a world system, and only international revolution can destroy it. That is why all revolutionary movements must seek to generalise and spread the struggle – from one section of the population to another, from one city to another, from one country to another. Only a worldwide upsurge of struggle and democracy from below can break the power of capital and the *global police state*.

The historical experience teaches us five critical lessons about the nature of mass revolutionary movements, and therefore about the nature of revolutionary agency:

- Organs of mass participatory democracy represent the embryonic form of an alternative popular state. They are an immediate and direct challenge to the power of capital and the existing repressive state apparatus. The co-existence of both in a revolutionary situation therefore creates an unsustainable 'dual power' – either the democracy smashes the existing state and establishes a new people's state, or the democracy will be smashed by counter-revolution.

- The democracy must be inclusive, participatory, and genuinely democratic, giving voice to the largest possible number of people, drawing in ever wider layers of the population, raising new demands as new forces join the struggle, always aiming to fan the flames of revolt into an irresistible firestorm of revolt from below.

- The 'rebel city' is the natural centre of revolutionary organisation, for here the working class is concentrated in great numbers and can achieve a critical social mass and political force. The workplaces, when taken over by the workers and run under workers' control, provide building-blocks of the democracy; but the building-blocks must be assembled into city-wide movements.

- The democracy must never look inwards, always outwards, never restrict itself to one district or city or country, but always think and act internationally. 'Socialism in one country' was the false ideology of Stalinist counter-revolution.

- The democracy must be able and willing to centralise its power, that is, to create joint committees, district assemblies, city-wide assemblies, ultimately a national co-ordination to seize state power and then to spread the revolution internationally. The power of capital and the state is highly centralised: the *democracy* of the working class must be centralised to defeat it.

10.

Democratic assemblies are essential to effective struggle for the following reasons: they allow the largest possible number of people to share ownership and control over the struggle; they raise consciousness and commitment through the fuller understanding achieved by collective discussion;

they increase confidence by bringing people together instead of leaving them isolated; they legitimise decision-making and encourage active participation; they create bonds of solidarity and mutual support. Democratic assemblies turn the masses in struggle into an active, participatory, practical *democracy*.

11.

Democracy in the sense used here is the embryo of a new social order, one where power flows upwards not downwards, where ordinary people are active decision-makers not passive election fodder, where the needs of the many become determinate.

The triumph of *democracy* requires the smashing of the state, the overthrow of capital, the restoration of *the commons*, and the transcendence of *alienation*.

12.

Between the late 19th and late 20th century, *democracy* took the primary form of trade-union organisation at the point of production. In British history, this 'trade-union century' was bracketed by two signal events, the victory of the London dockers in 1889, which launched a wave of unionisation among the semi-skilled and unskilled, and the defeat of the miners in 1984-5, after which union membership halved, workplace organisation disintegrated, and the union bureaucracies morphed into lobbyists and providers of personal services.

The decline of traditional trade unionism has created an organisational vacuum and given recent protest movements a distinctive character.

13.

The decline of traditional trade unionism will not be reversed. It depended upon relative geographical and social stability in earlier phases of capitalist development. Working-class communities grew up around particular industries located in particular towns and regions. Workers often spent their entire lives working in the local colliery, yard, mill, or factory. Sometimes several generations would follow suit. Communities were deep-rooted, with strong local ties based on family and neighbours, pubs and clubs, union membership and party allegiance.

Modern working-class experience is quite different. Transnational corporations comprise globalised concentrations of capital of unprecedented size. Their operations extend across scores of countries. Capital turns over at exceptional speed and is highly mobile. Financialised, digitalised, and outsourced, capital is more fluid than ever before. National, regional, and local capitals are subordinate to the dominant, ultra-mobile, market-controlling transnational fraction.

Outsourced production is less concentrated and stable. Contracts may or may not be renewed. If there is successful struggle in Dhaka, production can be relocated to Vietnam or Indonesia.

The working class becomes ever more precarious. A billion people are displaced and a billion and a half live in the slums of the Global South. Geographically and socially insecure, clinging to low-wage sweatshop jobs in the face of competition from thousands of unemployed, subject to long hours of exhausting toil and relentless management intimidation, workers are able to build workplace union organisation only with exceptional difficulty.

In the Global North, too, precarity is a pandemic. It means insecurity, overwork, low pay, high levels of stress, and constant management surveillance and bullying. The archetypal big workplace today is the union-free Amazon warehouse or Glasgow call-centre. Most of Britain's six million trade unionists are now in the public sector; but what they belong to are less organs of mass struggle than bureaucracies of lobbyists, lawyers, negotiators, and personal advisors.

14.

The mass movements of the neoliberal era, especially of the last 25 years, from the anti-globalisation and anti-war movements to Extinction Rebellion and Black Lives Matter, have been essentially protest movements. They have occasionally swelled into massive, even semi-insurrectionary movements, capable of waging ferocious street battles over many weeks, in a few cases powerful enough to topple a dictator. But there is not a single example of a completed popular revolution, where the existing state apparatus is destroyed, the rule of capital terminated, and a new order based on democracy, equality, and human need established.

The mass movements of the neoliberal era have had the following characteristics: 1) they have been essentially mass protest movements, not class-struggle movements with the potential to fight for state power; 2) they have not given rise to organs of democracy from below able to sustain and escalate the struggle, drawing in ever wider layers of the popular masses; 3) they have therefore followed a similar trajectory, up like a rocket, down like a stick, with the movement eventually subsiding through exhaustion and frustration, having failed to draw into the struggle a majority of the working class, the oppressed, and the poor; and 4) they have lacked the reserves, the strength, and the staying-power necessary to smash the state and end the rule of capital.

15.

Autonomism is both a reflection of the character of these movements and a legitimation and rein-forcement of that character. Social shallowness and political weakness are twins.

Autonomism eschews centralised organisation and makes a virtue of fragmentation and small-group independence and initiative. It sees large centralised organisations as bureaucratic, hierar-chical, and top-down, and counterposes au-tonomous organisation as a more democratic, participatory, bottom-up alternative.

In fact, in so far as mass protest arises from the initiative of small autonomous groups, what hap-pens is that the mass of protestors is disempow-ered. Instead of rank-and-file democracy, we have secretive cabals of self-appointed organisers. This has been described – correctly – as 'the tyranny of structurelessness'.

Real class struggle never has this organisational form. It gives rises to organs of open, inclusive, participatory, rank-and-file democracy, in which the masses in struggle become active decision-makers. Real class struggle requires the democratic forms necessary for the self-emancipation of the working class, the oppressed, and the poor.

16.

Revolution is an existential imperative, but, despite hundreds of millions engaged in militant street protest across the world, the masses have not yet constituted themselves as a revolutionary agent, that is, organised themselves in organs of participatory democracy in the context of class struggle from below. The crisis of the early 21st century is the crisis of revolutionary organisation.

Revolution from Below

1.

The revolution is an existential imperative, but a revolutionary situation does not yet exist.

The ecological and social crisis is deep, accelerating, and potentially catastrophic. The capitalist system – based on capital accumulation and exponential growth – is set to destroy human civilisation. The state is a militarised police state which exists to protect private property and corporate power. Bourgeois politics has therefore been reduced to mere *spectacle*. The dissonance between human need and political action is absolute.

But the great majority – the workers, the oppressed, and the poor, who are 90% of humanity

– have not yet become an active, organised, mobilised revolutionary force. The slide to oblivion therefore continues.

2.

The consciousness, confidence, and combativeness of the masses is always uneven. The masses do not all move into action at once. Revolutions are initiated and led by revolutionary vanguards.

The soldiers of the New Model Army were the vanguard of the English Revolution. The Parisian *sansculottes* were the vanguard of the French Revolution. The Petrograd *proletariat* were the vanguard of the Russian Revolution.

The spontaneous mass youth uprisings of the last two decades show the potential for new revolutionary vanguards to emerge in the crisis of the early 21st century. And in some cases, in the context of urban uprisings, we have seen embryonic forms of mass grassroots democratic organisation emerge. Again, the forms of a possible alternative future can be discerned in contemporary struggle.

3.

Revolution is like a mechanism of cog-wheels, where small wheels set in motion medium ones, and these set in motion larger ones, until the masses as a whole are in motion.

The role of activists is to engage with fighting vanguards. The example of fighting vanguards can inspire wider layers to join the struggle. The aim should always be to deepen and spread the struggle.

4.

First is the deed. Talk changes nothing. To act is to change social reality, to disrupt the existing order, to open up new possibilities. It is necessary to act. The job of revolutionaries is to make the revolution. The job of revolutionaries is therefore to work as part of the vanguard to raise the level and effectiveness of mass collective action, and to spread the action of the vanguard to wider layers of the working class, the oppressed, and the poor.

5.

The mass uprisings of the recent past have been mainly revolts of urban youth. Sometimes these have drawn into action whole sections of the working class, the oppressed, and the poor. Often they have reached near-insurrectionary levels, with violent confrontation with state forces sustained over many weeks.

The implication is that the modern metropolis will be the primary locus of revolutionary struggle in the period ahead. This reflects the nature of the modern working class: the fact that it is now overwhelmingly urbanised; and the fact that it is difficult to build strong workplace organisation. Neither rural guerrillas nor unionised workers, but, in the context of modern neoliberal capitalism, the street-fighters of the urban mass represent the potential revolutionary vanguard.

The modern capitalist city is a concentrated expression of the social crisis – a place where private greed and public squalor, grotesque wealth and obscene poverty, the rich and the poor are found cheek by jowl.

The modern capitalist city is also the place

where the largest numbers of youth, workers, oppressed, and poor can be most easily organised and mobilised to challenge the power of capital and the state.

The rebel city is the revolutionary vanguard conceptualised geographically.

6.

This does not mean that all the existing organisations – the trade unions, the (former) social-democratic parties, the campaign groups – are irrelevant. It means we must distinguish sharply between the leaderships and structures of these organisations – either bureaucratic, fossilised, sclerotic, a barrier to the development of struggle from below, or self-appointed, secretive, cabalistic, unwilling to reach out to widen the struggle – and the large numbers of people active within them. The audience for revolutionaries is never the leadership, but always the rank-and-file.

So it is right for revolutionaries to be involved in existing unions, parties, campaigns, protests, etc.

This is where they meet people who want to fight, people who can be won to the necessity for international red-green revolution from below – and therefore to a far more radical politics than that offered by the existing organisations.

7.

To transform protest into struggle, it will be necessary to establish organs of mass democracy inside the rebel city, to contest police control of the streets, to begin to take over urban infrastructure, to move towards the creation of autonomous zones where the authority of the state is blocked, the prerogatives of capital usurped, and popular power begins to develop.

If isolated and limited, such initiatives will be smashed by police action. So the aim must always be to generalise the struggle, to spread it to other areas, to draw in wider layers of the masses.

The *global police state* will meet such popular struggle with escalating levels of repressive violence, so it will be necessary to organise for self-defence – to set up committees of defence and armed defence militias.

There are numerous historical examples of mass urban uprisings defeating the bourgeois state and creating liberated zones under popular control – the Paris Commune of 1871, Budapest in 1919, Barcelona in 1936, Derry in 1969, many others. What is critical to the argument here is that such liberated zones cannot be seen as ends in themselves, but must be part of an ongoing revolutionary process. On the one hand, they provide zones where immediate revolutionary changes can be implemented – abolition of rents and landlordism, free public transport, takeover of empty property, workers' control of workplaces, housing of the homeless, organisation of food supplies, price controls, decommissioning of SUVs, anti-pollution and low-carbon measures, takeover of private health facilities, etc. On the other – and more importantly – they are platforms from which the revolution can be spread.

Capital and the state will meet this challenge with economic blockades and police attacks. The *global police state*, sometimes backed by fascist militias, will confront urban uprisings with militarised violence. Thousands of protesters have been murdered by the *global police state* across the world in the last two decades. Liberated zones will eventually be crushed if they stand still. Those who half make a revolution merely dig their own graves.

8.

What signs are there that the mass movements of the present can generate organs of popular democracy capable of transforming protest into revolution?

We start with a weak social base. In discussing the class struggle, Gramsci used a military metaphor and distinguished between 'a war of position' and 'a war of movement'. The trench war stalemate on the Western Front of 1914-1918 could be described as a war of position, the German *blitzkrieg* in Northern France in May/June 1940 as a war of movement. Equally, the powerful workplace-based labour movements built up during what I have described as 'the trade-union century' (late 19th to late 20th century) gave rise to protracted wars of position, in which organised workers were pitted again and again against the forces of capital and the state. But 40 years of defeat and retreat during the neoliberal era have broken the back of the international labour movement; and this we must recognise as a victorious war of movement by the ruling class and the repressive states. Class identity and solidarity, embodied in family, community, union, and party, have been severely eroded in the context of neoliberal atomisation and *alienation*. The recovery of revolutionary agency will involve a long process of building new class-based forms of organisation and resistance.

There are some straws in the wind. I will cite three examples. The *Plataforma de Afectados por la Hipoteca* (PAH) (Platform for People Affected by Mortgages) was set up in Barcelona in February 2009 during the wave of struggle triggered by the 2008 financial crisis. Over the next ten years, it established 220 branches across Spain. PAH took direct action to stop evictions and campaigned for rent reductions and state aid for residents unable to keep up with their mortgage payments. PAH stopped more than 2,000 evictions and its most prominent leader, Ada Colau, was elected Mayor of Barcelona. PAH is a clear example of class-based, bottom-up community resistance to the rule of capital and the authority of the state.

The Autonomous Administration of North and East Syria – *aka* Rojava – was established in 2012 in the context of the Syrian Civil War. In opposition to the Assad dictatorship, Turkish military aggression, and sectarian warlord militias, most notably the fascists of ISIS (Islamic State of Iraq and Syria), it has successfully defended much of its territory and built a popular state based on mass participatory democracy and committed to decentralisation of power, ecological sustainability, gender equality, and complete racial and religious tolerance. The region is home to a diverse population of ethnic Kurds, Arabs, Assyrians, Turkmen, Armenians, Circassians, and Yazidis. The Rojava 'Commune' has proved a haven for the oppressed in a world of murderous chaos and sectarianism.

Following the Sudanese Revolution of 2018-19, a mass popular movement has bubbled into existence. Among countless other grassroots organisations, the new resistance committees are of central importance. Originally the organs of the radical youth who formed the revolutionary vanguard, they have since expanded into a national network of neighbourhood resistance committees that have formed in major cities and rural communities. In the Bahri suburb of Khartoum, for example, there are believed to be 80 such committees, each with several hundred members.

There are other examples. The lesson is clear. The mass movements of the 2020s can give rise to organs of popular power and participatory democracy; that is, they have the potential to achieve revolutionary agency.

But this will not be done through spontaneity and autonomism. It represents a perspective and a strategy that must be fought for by revolutionaries active inside the mass movements; clear-sighted and strong-willed revolutionaries who refuse to accommodate to the autonomist and reformist politics of other activists.

9.

The smallest cog in the mechanism of revolution is the organisation of revolutionary activists.

The revolutionaries must be organised. Not into a sect of 50, 100, 250 that spends its time squabbling with other sects, equally small, equally irrelevant, each defining itself in opposition to the others in terms of petty differences, each under the direction of some sort of guru or clique. The revolutionary organisation should be broad, inclusive, open, tolerant of difference and debate, indeed thriving through the clash of ideas. It should comprise all those who understand the existential imperative of revolution, who value the lessons of the last 250 years of the class struggle, and who seek to unite theory and practice in an active struggle to change the world.

10.

Theory without practice is impotent. Practice without theory is blind. The unity of theory and practice makes revolution possible.

Revolutionary theory is the concentrated essence of 250 years' experience of the class struggle against capitalism.

Revolutionary theory must become a political force. To do this, it must become embedded in the revolutionary vanguard, especially among the urban youth of Generation Z and in the spontaneous uprisings of the rebel city.

For this to happen, revolutionary theory must itself be organised. Theory becomes an active historical force only when the revolutionaries – those who understand the existential imperative of revolution and who apply the lessons of 250 years of past struggles to contemporary practice – create an organisation rooted in the fighting vanguard.

The world crisis is the crisis of revolutionary theory and revolutionary organisation.

To save humanity and the planet, we need an organisation of revolutionaries committed to smashing the state, ending the rule of capital, and placing power in the hands of the people. The alternative is barbarism and extinction.

Pull-quotes

First we made things. Then we only consumed things. Now we merely observe things. From producer to consumer to spectator: this is the anthropological history of human *alienation* under the domination of capital.

Bourgeois politics has become form without substance, performance without action, *spectacle* without meaning. It has become a façade of images where the representation has no referent, no relationship with anything concrete, material, practical. There is only spin. A kaleidoscope of *spectacles*, signifying nothing.

Revolution has become an existential imperative for humanity and the planet. But the popular masses are yet to achieve revolutionary agency. Therefore, at present, we continue the slide towards oblivion. The term for this chronic condition of crisis and deadlock combined is *stasis*.

The internet becomes an immaterial world of virtual lives constructed of electronic bric-a-brac; a world of totally immersive *alienation* where nothing is done, nothing is made, where no real human relations are formed, no practical action performed, where *species-being* reduces to zero.

The existing bourgeois state apparatus is both the primary agent of *creeping fascism* and the local franchise of the *global police state*. Mass surveillance, repressive laws, militarised police, and nationalist-racist ideology herald a new *totalitarianism*.

The restoration of *the commons* has become an existential imperative. This can be achieved only by the overthrow of the *global police state*, the dispossession of the rich, the halting of capital accumulation, and the creation of a new democratic order. It can be achieved only by ending of human *alienation*. It can be achieved only by an international revolution of the working class, the oppressed, and the poor.

Democracy is the embryo of a new social order, one where power flows upwards not downwards, where ordinary people are active decision-makers not passive election fodder, where the needs of the many become determinate. The triumph of *democracy* requires the smashing of the state, the overthrow of capital, the restoration of *the commons*, and the transcendence of *alienation*.

The world crisis is the crisis of revolutionary theory and revolutionary organisation. To save humanity and the planet, we need an organisation of revolutionaries committed to smashing the state, ending the rule of capital, and placing power in the hands of the people. The alternative is barbarism and extinction.

WHAT IS A*CR

Anti*Capitalist Resistance is an organisation of revolutionary socialists. We believe red-green revolution is necessary to meet the compound crisis of humanity and the planet.

We are internationalists, ecosocialists, and anti-capitalist revolutionaries. We oppose imperialism, nationalism, and militarism, and all forms of discrimination, oppression, and bigotry. We support the self-organisation of women, Black people, disabled people, and LGBTQI+ people. We support all oppressed people fighting imperialism and forms of apartheid, and struggling for self-determination, including the people of Palestine.

We favour mass resistance to neoliberal capitalism. We work inside existing mass organisations, but we believe grassroots struggle to be the core of effective resistance, and that the emancipation of the working class and the oppressed will be the act of the working class and the oppressed ourselves.

We reject forms of left organisation that focus exclusively on electoralism and social-democratic reforms. We also oppose top-down 'democratic-centralist' models. We favour a pluralist organisation that can learn from struggles at home and across the world.

We aim to build a united organisation, rooted in the struggles of the working class and the oppressed, and committed to debate, initiative, and self-activity. We are for social transformation, based on mass participatory democracy.

info@anticapitalistresistance.org
www.anticapitalistresistance.org

ABOUT RESISTANCE BOOKS

Resistance Books is a radical publisher of internationalist, ecosocialist, and feminist books. We publish books in collaboration with the International Institute for Research and Education in Amsterdam (www.iire.org) and the Fourth International (www.fourth.international/en). For further information, including a full list of titles available and how to order them, go to the Resistance Books website.

info@resistancebooks.org
www.resistancebooks.org

9 780902 869356